MR. S

by Dan Zevin

Illustrated by Dylan Klymenko

THREE RIVERS PRESS
NEW YORK

Mr. Selfie had a good self-image.

In fact, he had tons of good self-images!

Every day, he took more and more.

And more.

He was self-sufficient, so he never asked
for help.

One night, he was getting ready for his date with Little Miss Tinder.

First, he shaved.

He started with his beard.

Then his mustache.

Then his pecs.

Next, he took a selfie of his favorite feature.

He was sure he had the biggest one in all the land.

Except for one small problem . . .

How was he supposed to fit the whole thing into one picture?

"Eureka!" Mr. Selfie exclaimed. "I will use my selfie stick for *my* selfie stick!"

"Should I send it on Snapchat?" he asked his FaceTime reflection.

"No," his reflection replied. "Your file is so large, it will never disappear."

"How about Insta? Wouldn't it look awesome with that Willow filter?"

"Totally," his reflection concurred. "But then it will go viral and you will be blamed by world leaders for breaking the Internet."

So he sexted the one person who'd appreciate it the most . . .

Himself!

One day, Mr. Selfie had a company-wide meeting.

It was his big chance to get noticed by the top brass.

First, he introduced himself to Little Miss VP.

Then, he made the acquaintance of Little Miss Senior VP.

And Little Miss *Executive* VP.

Finally, he met Mr. President!

Soon he was asked to clean out his desk by Little Miss HR.

This can mean only one thing, Mr. Selfie knew.

They are moving me to a splendid corner office with a skyline view.

"Can I move in immediately?" he inquired. "I need a new selfie for LinkedIn."

ME
CEO

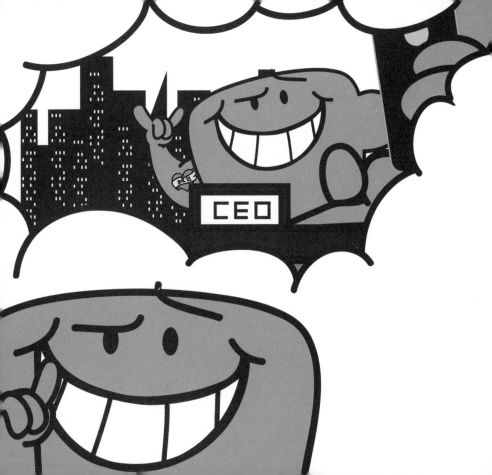

And then he was escorted out by security.

When Monday came, Mr. Selfie was so happy he'd gotten fired.

There were places to go, people to meet, selfies to take!

First, it was off to Afghanistan for an action-packed shot behind enemy lines.

Next stop: the Swiss Alps, for some daredevil downhills on the Matterhorn.

As soon as he got home, he went to his favorite local selfie spot.

The gym!

He warmed up by shooting a Vine of his seven-pack.

Then he did his upside-down kettlebell swings.

He could really see results.

1,228 loops in five minutes!

ME

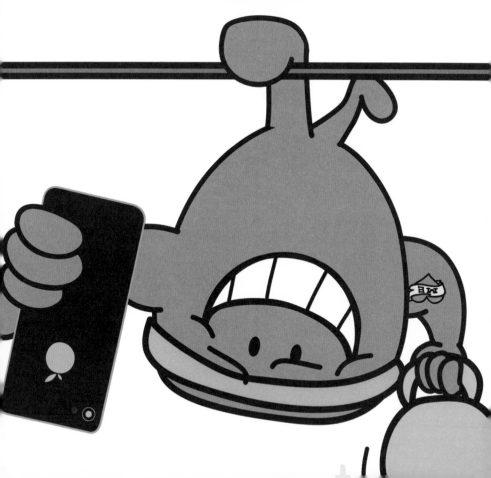

One day, Mr. Selfie set off for the zoo.

He went straight to the most photogenic animal he could find.

It was Jo-Jo, the man-eating wildebeest.

He could have asked someone to take his picture with Jo-Jo in the background.

But that would be too risky, wouldn't it?

He knew that talking to strangers was dangerous.

They might shoot his chin from the wrong angle.

ME

To play it safe, he jumped into Jo-Jo's cage to get the shot himself.

But there was just one problem.

Jo-Jo was camera shy.

Extremely.

Later, a kindly doctor checked his vital signs.

And Mr. Selfie checked his Facebook.

At that moment, he felt like one lucky fellow.

His sympathy selfie was killing it!

Mr. Selfie had lost a leg, yet he'd gained something far more valuable.

A sh*tload of Likes.

●●●○○ AT&T
News Feed
Status
Photo
Check In
Mister Selfie shared a photo
15 min
000,000,000,000
1,095,112,000,000,000,000,000,000,
000,000,000,000,000,000,000,
000,000,000,000,000,000,000,
000,000,000,000,000,000,000,
000,000,000,000,000,000,000,
000,000,001 people like this

Published in the United States by Three Rivers Press, an imprint of the
Crown Publishing Group, a division of Penguin Random House LLC, New York.
www.crownpublishing.com

THREE RIVERS PRESS and the Tugboat design are registered trademarks of
Penguin Random House LLC.

Library of Congress Cataloging-in-Publication Data is available upon request.

ISBN 978-1-101-90447-3
eBook ISBN 978-1-101-90459-6

PRINTED IN CHINA

Illustrations by Dylan Klymenko
Cover design by Dylan Klymenko

10 9 8 7 6 5 4 3 2 1

First Edition